IF I SAY

If I Say

J. Renee

IF I SAY
COPYRIGHT © 2021 BY JALYNN RENEE.
ALL RIGHTS RESERVED.
NO PART OF THIS BOOK MAY BE REPRODUCED IN ANY FORM
WITHOUT WRITTEN PERMISSION FROM THE AUTHOR.

DESIGN & LAYOUT BY R. CLIFT
ILLUSTRATIONS BY JULIA DREAMS

ISBN: 978-0-578-97805-5

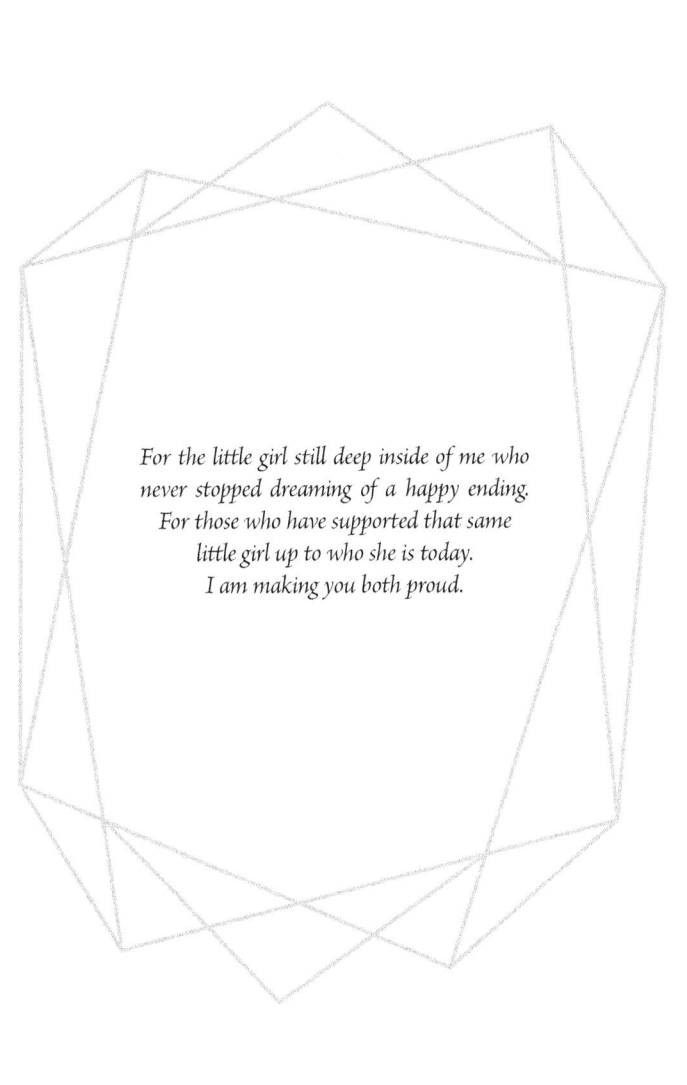

For the little girl still deep inside of me who never stopped dreaming of a happy ending. For those who have supported that same little girl up to who she is today. I am making you both proud.

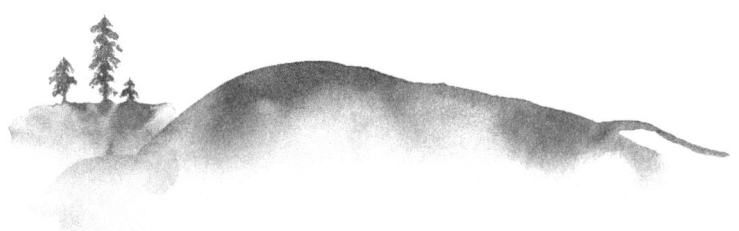

A few words about the little girl in these poems;

When I first thought about writing out all the feelings that have stuck with me over the years, I thought about going down the traditional 'write and burn' path. They were my feelings after all. Why would anyone else want to read about the depths of my mind? Then I found the poetry community online and I finally felt like my inner feelings belonged somewhere. A place that I could relate to others inside their pieces, and a place for someone else to get lost inside my own as well.

While the first two sections might be a tough ride through personal trauma and a rocky road to who I am today, the third and final section is for you, my darling reader. It is left to give you the hope and motivation to know that even through the worst days, you will always make it out on the other side with knowledge and growth.

Inside each one of these pages, you will find yourself immersed inside past memories of an absent father, a loss of a dear friend, heartache from past relationships, and the aftermath of certain life situations. You will also find yourself stumbling through my daily life dealing with leftover trauma, feelings of failure and competition, and fear of the future plans my life holds. However, you are left with a little sunshine at the end of our ride.

With that being said, the story is now being passed to you. Hold it dearly, for you now hold my entire heart.

WHO YOU ONCE WERE

WHO YOU HAVE BECOME

WHO YOU ARE MEANT TO BE

IF I SAY

Even as I sat
in the back corner
of that bar alone,
I was reminded of
what you once promised me.

*a simple life full of
happiness and peace.*

The world says you
are never ready
to lose someone so
dear to your heart,
but my darling...

*nothing could have
prepared me to
lose you so young.*

IF I SAY

You taught me that
love is a losing game
when only

*one person is
playing along.*

J. RENEE

Oh, how quickly you
forgave and dismissed
your faulty actions

*as if they affected
you at all.*

IF I SAY

The thing about
careless words is
that once they
fall past your lips

*they last a
lifetime inside
someone else's mind.*

I might have set my
bar a little too high,
and expected a little too
much from a man
who could not

*look me in the eye
while he spat his
honest words my way.*

IF I SAY

All along I thought it was
my choice who I let in,
who I let consume
all that I am, but then

*you came around and
claimed that choice
as your own.*

I never pictured myself
being the one to
pick up habits from those
around me,
but once I found my lips
pressed to a bottle at
3 AM

*I realized you rubbed
off on me more
than I thought you would.*

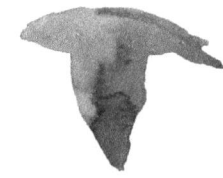

IF I SAY

You left me with the
pain of a child
that grew up entirely
too fast

*against her will
and suffering without
the guidance
you were meant to give.*

J. RENEE

Did you picture me
for a fool?
Did you think you
could crawl into the
depths of my heart and

*make me love you
with hopes alone?*

They warned me
that you would
leave me covered in
darkness

is it my fault
I saw your light?

J. RENEE

Darling, you could have
written me a
symphony, but

*all you left me with
was silence.*

IF I SAY

They thought I would
stay calm
and silent until
the end

*until the fire
inside my soul
roared to life.*

I have wandered
through the relentless
seas of fire

*yet I still feel
just as
burned as before.*

IF I SAY

The collision of our
two mixed souls
shook the universe
to its core

*setting fire to the
entire galaxy
in our loving wake.*

J. RENEE

I never could
quite figure you out
the moment I
met you

*and maybe that
was a
blessing draped
in a daydream.*

IF I SAY

I have never known
a need for
hunger like your
dying love

taking and pulling
at the meat
from my bones
in time.

Your heart laid
claim to the broken
pieces of
myself

your hands
crafting the sharp
edges back
together.

IF I SAY

The love you poured
into the depths
of my drought
filled veins

*pulled me under
with a sweet
taste like
cherry wine.*

J. RENEE

I may have lost
the person I wanted
to be in the
past

*with that being said,
there is a divine
feeling to this
bliss.*

IF I SAY

Was it wrong
of my heart to want
you all to
myself?

*was it wrong
of my mind to think
that you were?*

Will this feeling of
absolute bliss
ever fade away
into the
abyss?

*or, will I forever
be drunk
on the thought
of you and I?*

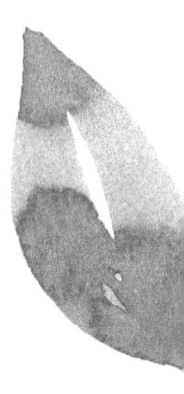

IF I SAY

I know you thought
that your actions
were harmless
in the
beginning

*did you know
they would leave
me feeling
numb for days
on end?*

Too many promises
left your mouth
to be completely
believable

*which is why
no one can believe
anything
from your tainted lips.*

If you could talk
to the person
I was years ago

*you would find
that she hardly
believed in much.*

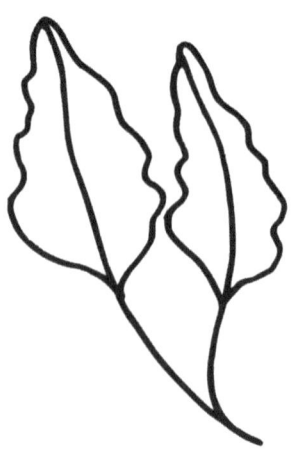

Closed off and
reserved
to anyone
I come close to

*I have been
going through the
motions with your
name on it.*

IF I SAY

I always believed
in anything
that came stumbling
out of your mouth

*I knew I should
have trusted my
sweet intuition
instead.*

Would you have
trusted me to
undress all that
you were on
the inside?

*all your fears,
anxious thoughts,
and battle wounds
out on display.*

IF I SAY

It is almost
magical how you
took every flaw
inside my mind

*making them
shake in their
boots at the thought
of having no
power over me
any longer.*

How did you think
that your words
would simply
stay between the
two of us?

*you have long
forgotten them,
while they will
echo inside
my subconscious
until my last day.*

IF I SAY

Did you know that
this illness
will never show its
head outside of mine?

*you will never
see what it
does to me on
the inside.*

J. RENEE

Counting all the times
you told me
that you would
leave

*honey, when do I
stop counting
now that you are
gone for good?*

If you want a
chance at seeing who
I can really be

*you have to
let go of
your hold on my soul.*

J. RENEE

I burned alive
inside each lie you
told on my behalf

*the voice of a child
crying out
through the flames.*

IF I SAY

Even though you
left me hungover
with your words
dripping like honey
against my memory

I would drink in
all that you
had to say over
and over again.

Tell me again
how your love is
the best medicine for
my heart

*remind me again
after I
overdose on
all of you.*

IF I SAY

I have been
stuck between
not wanting your
love at all

*and wanting to
let it consume all
that I have left.*

J. RENEE

It is a constant
battle inside my
head

*wanting to move
to the future
and
wanting to live
comfortably in
the past.*

IF I SAY

You once asked me
what I thought
about intimacy

*if only you knew
it was the little
moments with you.*

Maybe I am the
one to blame for
skipping past those
signs

*maybe I was
out of line
for trusting someone
like you.*

The sun rose
above the horizon
today
and for the
first time

*I felt at
peace with
myself.*

I listen for
your siren song
inside the
waves crashing at
my feet,
letting it draw
me in and

*allowing it to
drown my soul
to the depths
of the dark.*

IF I SAY

I wonder why
I cannot seem to
fall asleep at
night with
little thoughts of
you racing through
my mind, but
then

*I remember once
the darkness
settles back inside
the corners of
my head.*

J. RENEE

Some nights I still
feel your
fragile touch
caress my tainted skin,
an unwanted
thought slipping
through my mind

*if only I could
blink it away
and let it
get lost inside
time once more.*

IF I SAY

If you ask me
how I am doing,
I would simply
say that I'm
getting by

*I have gotten
good at
lying, haven't I?*

I pride myself
in knowing that
you will never
find a soul like
mine in your
search to
move on.
I am one being

*one singular soul
that is
unique in a
million different ways.*

IF I SAY

How do you
give up
hoping that someday
they might
care about you
the way you
desperately want
them to?

*how do you
let go
of the person
you wish they
would be?*

I would like to
say that I am
dancing on your
grave
with a
twisted smile

*my lips turned up
at the corners
for the first time
since knowing you.*

IF I SAY

I thought that
I would recognize
the familiar face
staring back at
myself
in that shattered
piece of glass
on the floor

*but I am
unrecognizable
even to
my own mind.*

At what point
do I stop
begging you for
the love
you leisurely
hand out to
everyone else?

*at what point
do I accept
that I
am nothing
to you?*

IF I SAY

I have been
breathing
with shallow breaths
as I chase
a vision of
my old self
through my
nightmares

*leaving it out
of reach
with each
hungover morning.*

If I could find
myself
amongst the
shelves
inside your mind

*I would read
about myself
for days.*

IF I SAY

You will find
the image
of who I once
was inside
the

*memories that I
have left
for you.*

J. RENEE

Written goodbyes
never seem
to stick
inside my heart

*so, darling
please
speak.*

IF I SAY

They all tell me
that you
love me in
your own way

but, I would be
better off
without your
love at all.

J. RENEE

Time after time,
I feel as if I may
never be good
enough

*but, your laughter
tells a
different story
entirely.*

IF I SAY

Out of all the
different versions of
Heaven I created

*the one where
you never leave
is my favorite.*

I can still remember
what it felt like
to love you

*perfectly imperfect
like the
warm Texas weather.*

IF I SAY

Most days I
cannot seem to
think a single
straight thought

*a blanket of anxiety
keeping my
mind warm.*

Take a look around
darling and
remember what life
used to be

*you used to have
a spark
for all that the
day gave.*

IF I SAY

There has always
been an
unbalanced force
of chaos
inside

*my mind and
soul a tangled
mess until the
end of time.*

Promise me that
if my soul
is ever consumed
by darkness

*you will come in
search of
what is left
of me.*

In the stillness of
all that you are
when you are
with me

*I found that
who I am
with you is who
I once lost.*

J. RENEE

Heaven and Hell
were taught to
my soul at a
young age

*and yet,
I still would
love you
if it meant
losing both.*

IF I SAY

I am wandering around
the wasteland
you have made

*the meaning of
your emotionless
apologies
wearing thin.*

Call it foolishness
if you would like,
just another
excuse for
my love

if I could,
I would pull away
and pretend
I was not
wrong.

IF I SAY

The sun peaked
behind the
hanging clouds
for the
first time in days

and somehow,
everything felt
right in the
world for once.

J. RENEE

The leaves outside
are changing
to a new season

*how foolish of
me to think
that we would
stay the
same.*

If you listen well,
you can hear the
mountains
pouring out praise

*for a woman
who once
belonged to the
crisp morning air.*

J. RENEE

Some call her
the devil in disguise,
a walking
contradiction

*but, what a title
for a woman
on a simple
mission.*

IF I SAY

For years and years
the ghost of
what we used to
be
floated around

*but, no more
I am releasing
that spirit
to a new world.*

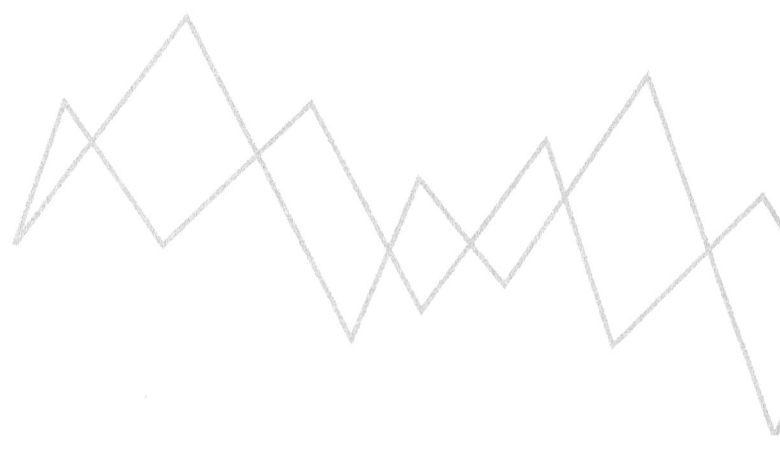

J. RENEE

I spent years
chasing after the
thought of you

*until today when
I finally moved
on to a
new day.*

IF I SAY

You can toss out
your hate filled
words,
call me selfish
if you want

*I don't give a damn
what you think
of me
any longer.*

J. RENEE

You can blame
it on the
empty bottles
of Whiskey
if you want

*even though we
both know that
is simply
not the
case at all.*

IF I SAY

If you had to ask
me where I
feel the most
safe
inside this
destruction

*I would say
inside your
soul
in a heartbeat,
my dear.*

J. RENEE

Loving all of you
was a religion
I was never prepared
to follow

*even now as you
pull me close
under the
same Heavens
you pray to.*

IF I SAY

When death comes
rearing its
ill-fated
gaze upon my
last day

*promise me that
you will
follow me in
my last breath.*

My mind is constantly
buzzing with
self destructive
thoughts

*sometimes drowning
in this pit
is better than
silence.*

IF I SAY

How do you tell
everyone around you
that you see
what they don't?

*how do you tell
them that you
hate what you see
in the
lying funhouse mirror?*

J. RENEE

No matter how
far you run,
no matter how
loud you speak

*you will never
be able to
shout over the
honest truth.*

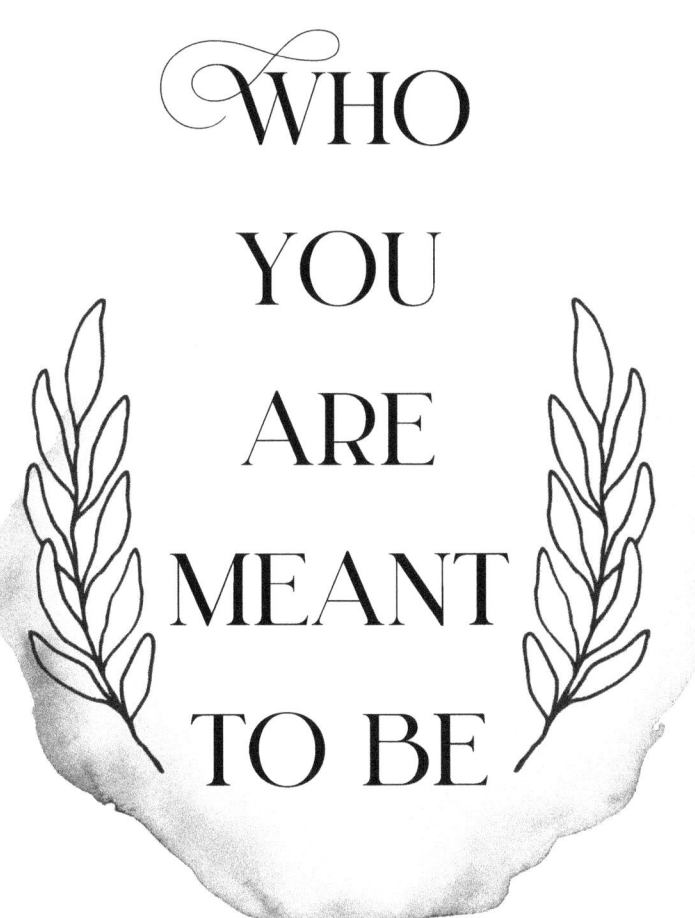

There are those days
that you want to
paint inside
your memories

*the days you
have been
begging the
universe to
bring to you.*

J. RENEE

There comes a day
when who you are
is like re-reading
a familiar
chapter in a book

and who you are
meant to be
is inside
the story
you have yet
to write.

IF I SAY

I stare at you
and wonder who
made you think
that you were
not meant
to take hold of
your own
soul

*I wonder when you
will wake up
and see that
no one knows
you much
like you do.*

J. RENEE

Much like the
hopeful sunshine
each morning
in the new sky

*you have to wake
with the
same strength
inside yourself.*

Life often gives us
grief that we
never imagined
we could take

*the way we move
through it all
is the real test.*

Your soul knows its
limits when you
have reached
the end

*let yourself
rest
and pick up
with a
new day
tomorrow.*

IF I SAY

Do not let them
quiet your laughter
or make you
hide your
happiness

*you deserve
every ounce of
bliss
running through
your veins.*

One day your hours
of self doubt
and
destructive
behavior will be
a distant memory

*a forgotten chapter
in the story
you are still
completing.*

You are deserving of
everything hanging
above the clouds

*everything under
your wandering
feet as well
if I am honest.*

J. RENEE

If you would let
your love
shine through the
cracks
in your soul

*you will find your
heart melting
with pure joy.*

IF I SAY

Once you have created
a life that
seems real to
your heart

*make sure it
resonates with your
ever growing soul.*

J. RENEE

> The sun will rise
> against all that
> you have been through

> *as you will,*
> *in due time*
> *when you are*
> *full of its rays.*

You will heal
from all that you
hold onto
each day

on your own time,
never on
their time or
expectations.

You will never hear
your own
outspoken voice
inside
someone else

*therefore, please
listen to
what your
inner voice
has to say.*

IF I SAY

No matter what
the depths of your
brain says
as it is
pulling you under

*you are not the
darkest parts
of your soul.*

No one on the
outside can
force you to
change inside
your own mind

*no one can
reveal to you
what to
do in your
own soul.*

You may think
you are still the
fragile person
they made you
think you were in
the beginning

*but, you have
grown into
something they
will never be
able to touch.*

I am done thinking
I will never reach
what I want

*from now on,
I am only
grabbing what is
meant to be.*

Make these days
the ones you
joke about in the
future

*the ones who thought
they could
ever hold you
back.*

J. RENEE

If I could do
anything in this
mess of my
growing years

*it would be to
convince you
that you
deserve this
life too.*

Thank you for diving into all I am and
reading along with all my feelings.

You have given my words a safe space and
for that, I will forever be grateful.

Please, never forget to live past all that you
have been through,
you are brave, darling.

Acknowledgements

To the person dear to my heart, Nana, thank you for always supporting each and every adventure I have taken that has led us here. This book came to be from your constant motivation and outward love.

To the other half of who I will always be, Mom, you have given me a life full of endless support and a space full of love and acceptance. I will forever be thankful for all that you have done to make me who I am now.

To those who have stayed by my side throughout the earliest ups and downs, Nikole and JJ, thank you for always encouraging me to continue working towards my future goals. You are so special to me.

To the man that has taken my heart and soul as his own, Rocky, you have taken every dream I have ever had and helped make them into reality with your endless love. My heart is yours forever.

About The Author

Jalynn Vinson is a writer and over-all dreamer of all things magical based at the tip top of Texas. She began her writing journey back in her younger years, and has now evolved into the poet she has become today. In fact, this book was written in just one short week. Those words poured out and did not stop.

She believes that when the timing is right, that is when things will move into play, with the exception of those times when you have to pick up a pen and write that future for yourself. Then, it is truly up to us.

www.ingramcontent.com/pod-product-compliance
Lightning Source LLC
Chambersburg PA
CBHW062051290426
44109CB00027B/2795